To Nellie with our very
best wishes on the occasion of
her birthday October 30th 1967.
Charlie and Edy the Wessel

The Many Faces

of Quebec

The Many

Faces

Text by Jean-Charles Harvey

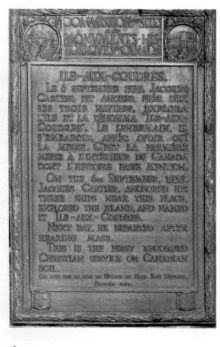

Translated by Alta Lind Cook

of Quebec

Photographs by Marcel Cognac

Designed by Pat Gangnon of
Leslie Smart & Associates Limited
Printed in Canada

8

The Many Faces of Quebec

Chapters

MACMILLAN OF CANADA / TORONTO
ST. MARTIN'S PRESS / NEW YORK

Originally published in 1964 by
Le Cercle du Livre de France

1

The Most Beautiful River

There can be few strangers who, entering Canada for the first time from the Atlantic and discovering the great waterway we call the St. Lawrence, do not experience a feeling of admiration and amazement. This peerless river may be said to have fathered Quebec. From 1608 to the present day it has never ceased to sustain, nurture, and delight its people. Without it this great province, three times the size of France, might still be a paradise for hunters, fishermen, and *coureurs de bois*; and in this vast land, once a wilderness, millions of French Canadians who today live on its shores would never have existed. In this sense Quebec is the child of the St. Lawrence.

We may wonder what dreams of future development came to the mind of the intrepid Jacques Cartier when, in that summer of 1535, his small ship carried him nearly six hundred miles along this navigable waterway from the open sea to the foot of Mount Royal – to the very spot where our metropolis of Montreal now stands. The year before, he had sailed along the coast of the Gaspé peninsula where he had planted a cross in the name of the King of France. And now with all sails spread to the wind he made his way along the marvellous

azure passage that would lead him to the heart of an immense continent. What wealth lay hidden behind those dark walls of rock and forest all along those endless shores battered by the waves or alive with the cries of countless seabirds? What manner of man would one day set out to conquer these mysteries? What kind of towns would arise in this awesome loneliness? What castles, what churches, what steeples would some day be reflected in these blue waters? To these questions that he undoubtedly put to himself the navigator from St. Malo would have replied, 'Here, sooner or later, France must come and sow her seed.

The fulfilment of this prophecy had to wait until 1608, when Champlain, borne along in his turn by the great river, came and founded Quebec. Cartier, Champlain, why are you not with us to see the results of your adventure? Instead of your small sailing vessels that took months to cross the Atlantic there are now ships of from twenty to thirty thousand tons which cover the distance from the sea to Montreal in no time to put down thousands of travellers and cargoes of every kind. Night and day the St. Lawrence is furrowed by steamships, cargo vessels, yachts, schooners, fishing boats. Many

16

of these ships, laden with merchandise, will go
upstream from the city and on through the
famous St. Lawrence Seaway to the head of
Lake Superior in the very heart of the continent,
returning to Europe laden with the products of
the Canadian soil and of Canadian industry.
Little more than three and a half centuries ago
it was the birch-bark canoe that made it possible
for the native tribes to survive, thanks to the
countless streams that led them from one fishing
and hunting territory to another. Now it is the
era of speed on land, on sea, and in the air. And
the great Montreal island, with Mount Royal
(so named by Cartier) towering over it, is still
a part of all this progress, thanks to the river
that ties it to all parts of the globe.

2

Montreal and Its Countryside

On the site of that Indian village to which Jacques Cartier came for the first time now stands one of the great cities of North America. Our historian François-Xavier Garneau wrote that the primitive establishment 'was made up of about fifty wooden dwellings fifty feet long and twelve to fifteen feet wide. Each house, whose outside walls were made of strips of bark cleverly sewn together, contained several rooms arranged around one large square room where the family gathered around the hearth. The village was surrounded by a triple palisade.'

Today we have the immense city which, along with its numerous suburbs, has a population of over two million inhabitants, the great majority French-speaking. Night and day it hums with life and activity, making one of those contrasts in history of which the New World offers so many examples.

A CITY IN PERPETUAL MOTION

At the foot of Mount Royal we can feel the pulse-beat of a whole nation. Over the concentration of trade, finance, entertainment, the pursuit of pleasure, the comings and goings of a cosmopolitan crowd, and various manifestations of art, giant skyscrapers rise, and here the activity of a people centres. Morning and evening in the rush hours there is the ebb and flow of masses of humanity going into and coming out of the big department stores and high buildings. Countless vehicles arriving from every direction, seemingly thrown into the streets all at once, obstruct the roads, fill the air with the roar of motors and the blare of horns, fall into a kind of impatient immobility, start off, stop again, and then finally, as if by a miracle, arrive somewhere – at the office, the store, or the workshop, or home again when the day is over. Later on in the evening another race towards the heart of the city begins, towards the lighted skyscrapers, towards the magical forest of many-coloured neon lights, towards the theatres, the movie houses, the sports arenas, and the night entertainment. Soon the crowd of merrymakers and tourists

22

23

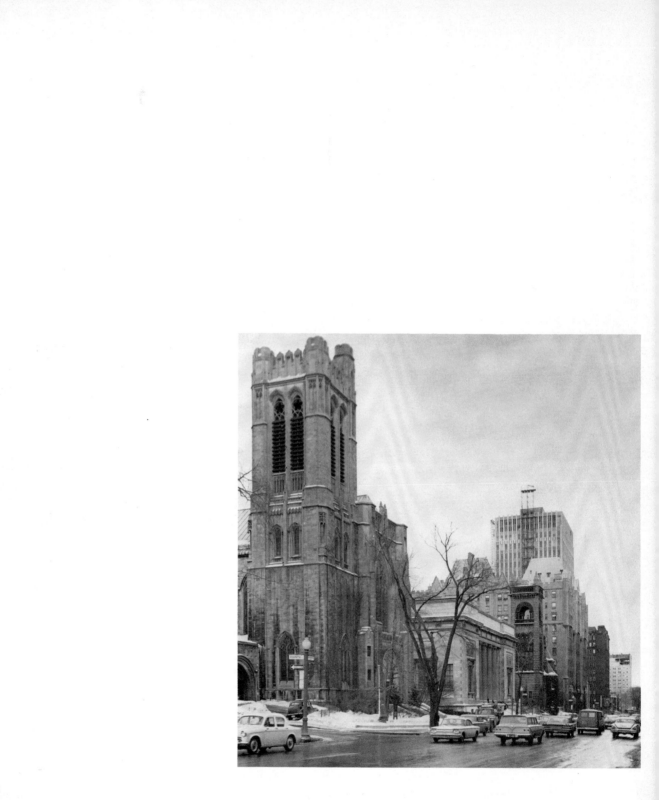

24

will fill the night-clubs where they will sing and dance, eat and drink, and where beautiful girls and glamorous performers create an atmosphere of relaxation and pleasure. And so Montreal gives the impression of a city that never sleeps, where the pleasures of night life take over when the work of the day ends.

THE CITY AT REST

Nevertheless, Montreal is something else. One has to leave the centre of the city to find this out. Its people live in districts that stretch north, south, east, and west from Mount Royal, where in thousands of homes they enjoy a happy family life, the television, and a good night's sleep. On the slope of the mountain in Outremont and Westmount there are luxurious dwellings where wealthy Montrealers prefer the quiet of home to the vibrant bustle of the centre of town. This whole sober society that controls the economic and social life of the city lives in the shadow of the impressive dome of a basilica and in the environment of two great universities. To this may be added the parks, oases of lawns, flowers, and trees that have risen as if by magic in the midst of the noise and smoke and commercial and industrial hubbub, as have the half-urban half-rural municipalities that encircle Montreal on the great island. Here we have the picture of an interesting and diverse humanity that gives character to this Canadian metropolis, second largest French-speaking city in the world.

It would have been impossible to choose a better place for the World's Fair of 1967. From historic St. Helen's Island, from the great display of the products of the civilized world, countless visitors will look on the city at night, illuminated and enchantingly reflected in the waters of the St. Lawrence; will look on ocean steamers gliding majestically under the Jacques Cartier bridge; and will perhaps be unable to keep from going back in mind to a distant past when the rugged sailors of St. Malo landed at the village of Hochelaga.

28

29

30

3

Jewel of America

Quebec City, the capital, rises on the rim of the St. Lawrence one hundred and seventy miles east of Montreal. People are fond of calling it the jewel of America. Nobody disputes the title. From the first moment of seeing it, Quebec City is immediately recognizable as one of the most beautiful cities in North America. Lying along a promontory, it is dominated by a citadel like a sentinel in stone that rises above it on the top of a lofty cliff. On clear mornings the sun dapples its forest of houses built in tiers along the steep slope of the cliff, the masonry of its centuries-old ramparts, the bell-towers of its basilica and churches, the imposing silhouette of its Château Frontenac, its university, and a whole lacework of old roofs outlined against the sky. Champlain, its founder, who chose it as the site of the first French colony, had been able at first sight to appreciate the beauty as well as the strategic importance of the promontory.

Here you are immersed in an atmosphere of Old France. The language that you hear spoken on every hand is French. Inside the fortified town, which is surrounded by a stone wall pierced by two granite gateways as if to make a common borderline between past and present, there are still a few narrow streets left just as

35

36

they were laid out in Montcalm's time, with centuries-old houses in Norman style and many relics of the early years of the colony. This very French appearance is often an astonishing discovery for the stranger, who is fortunate to have found a few pages of the history of North America that are too often left unread.

There is nobody more hospitable, more sociable than the citizen of Quebec City. He has retained a remnant of that Latin vivacity that contrasts with the British reserve. If you want to see this for yourself, stroll along Dufferin Terrace at nightfall on a summer day. This is a vast promenade where people flock from all directions, men and women of every age and condition and gait. They come in crowds, full of life, to walk up and down, up and down, on the immense wooden platform hanging on the side of that precipitous rock. It is like a balcony for the whole city: smiling young couples hand in hand, groups of chattering students, solemn and dignified elderly men discussing politics between puffs of their cigars; tourists casting curious glances at this crowd where everybody seems to know everybody else. Then, turning your back on this spectacle of a city out for a stroll, go and lean on the railing and just look. What a pano-rama! At your feet is the Lower Town, with its streets so narrow that automobiles do not dare to venture in, with its ancient chapel of Notre-Dame-des-Victoires; and skirting it, lapping at the wharves, is the St. Lawrence, where ferry boats cross between the two banks and the great steamships with their red funnels glide slowly by. Over there towards the east lies the fabulous Island of Orleans where you will go tomorrow to see a manor house, and tall stone houses with painted roofs and several chimneys, and churches decorated with sculptures in wood. To the left there is the St. Charles River, spanned by many bridges that allow thousands of vehicles to come and go. Away in the distance there is the impressive mass of Cape Tourmente that falls straight down into the St. Lawrence, while behind it the range of the Laurentians stretches to infinity.

THE CALÈCHE AND ITS DRIVER

Perhaps you will be tempted to take a *calèche* to see Quebec City. This attractive horse-drawn carriage, because of its leisurely pace, allows you to get a better look at things. Your driver will be a middle-aged coachman with a heavy moustache who knows his town by heart from having

37

acted as guide to a host of visitors. In his piercing eyes, which enliven his weather-beaten face, there is a great shrewdness. A talkative fellow and a scoffer, he will tell you about his wife and his ten children and about his hunting and fishing adventures; he will make jokes at the expense of his prime minister, his member of parliament, and his curé; and then, with a shout to his horse – *hue! dia!* – off he goes with you across the city. On the way he will want you to admire the only French-speaking parliament in America, then several monuments, especially a bronze group of Indians looking at themselves in the clear water of a fountain. After that he will take you to the Plains of Abraham where he will recount in his own way the story of the famous battle in which Wolfe and Montcalm died and the fate of Canada was sealed for centuries to come. He will take you into the vice-regal estate, the Bois de Coulonge, the traditional residence of the representative of Her Majesty the Queen. Then he will drive you back to the old city, through the Porte Saint-Jean that marks the boundary between old and new, until slowly, dangerously, the *calèche* plunges and bumps down towards the Lower Town and its historical treasures.

Champlain's town is as lively in winter as it is in summer, perhaps more so. The Quebec *Carnaval* is said to be the most important event of its kind in the world. While thousands of skiers meet in the forest-clad mountains to the north, the city overflows with visitors. The palace, the monuments, and the statues, all carved in ice, and the splendid festivities in hotels and night-clubs are added attractions. Mardi Gras is the time of the famous parade of dramatic floats, giant creatures with great false heads, patriotic societies, and the great crowd whose mad merriment is communicated to the entire city. The whole thing ends with a marvellous display of fireworks – all of it delighting the hundred thousand visitors who have come from all over Canada (especially from Montreal) and from many foreign lands.

In short, at any time of the year Quebec City is the most authentic expression of French life in North America.

41

45

4

Across Country

As soon as we leave the principal cities of the province of Quebec we are in the world of nature and are conscious of that immensity in the midst of which man can enjoy, more than anywhere else, plenty of air to breathe and light to work by. For his physical well-being there is the very atmosphere of freedom.

THE TYPICAL VILLAGE

To explore the Quebec countryside let us choose, if you like, a sunny summer day. Excellent roads run everywhere through the inhabited areas. As far as the eye can see on either side of the grey roadway there are trees bedecked with green: maples, firs, birches, elms, poplars. Here and there a modern bridge spans a river or quick-flowing stream. To right and left are fields under cultivation or short stretches of woods, herds of cattle, flocks of sheep, farm-houses, and a few miles ahead a church steeple. And soon you will be in a typical French-Canadian village. Standing high in the very centre of it is the church, more often than not imitation gothic, with statues of the saints sheltered in niches on its wide façade. Right beside it there will be an impressively large presbytery where the curé, wearing his biretta, may be seen walking back and forth

49

on the wide verandah reading his prayer book. Across the way is the convent where you catch a glimpse of the winged coifs of some teaching nuns. Further along is a boys' school with a big yard where reverend brothers in their cassocks are taking part in the boys' games.

Each village has its main street with its general store – the rendezvous for men who have nothing to do and who go there to talk politics or play a game of checkers – its town hall, its fire-hall, and a double row of houses buzzing with the children of this extremely prolific society.

The architecture is noticeably different from that of the other provinces and of the northern United States, where every house is separated from the road by a carefully mowed lawn and is surrounded by a well-clipped hedge. French-Canadian homes, which may look very unlike each other, are usually set right at the sidewalk and near together, apparently to allow for neighbourly conversation from one window to another. The extreme sociability of French Canadians shows up in this arrangement.

In the majority of houses constructed recently, where red brick and wood predominate, there is perhaps no apparent over-all plan or very definite style, but you get the undefinable impres-

50

52

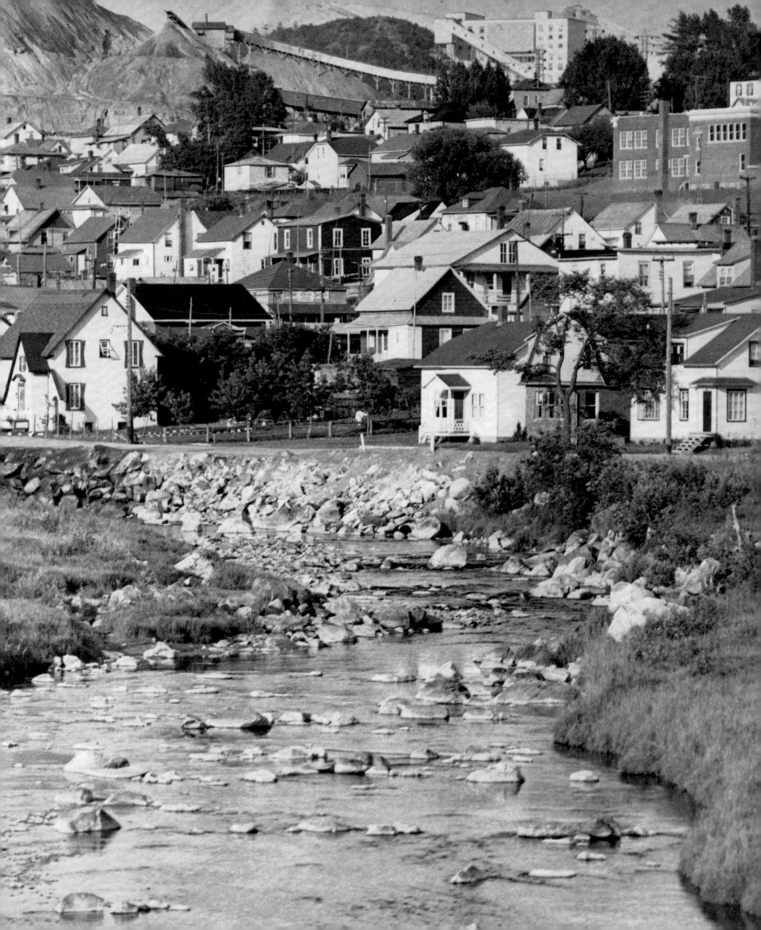

sion of a deep intensity of life, a kind of warmth that comes from a multiplicity of close contacts in a group of people united by the same ideas and the same beliefs.

In these rural centres, notably around Montreal and Quebec City, you will admire a few old stone houses dating back more than a century. In their massive masonry and in their harmonious lines they are the handsome last witnesses to an architectural heritage. As you go along, a good guide will point out some of our former manor houses where the gentry of New France used to live. According to the archivist Pierre-Georges Roy, they symbolize the soul of a whole people. Our *seigneurs* built little castles for themselves on their rural estates. To be sure, their manors did not have the appearance of medieval fortresses. They were simply great houses built of field stone held together by good mortar. The main body of the house was in one long rectangular construction; sometimes wings decorated with small towers were added at both ends. Unfortunately these last visible reminders of French rule in Canada have often been allowed to fall into ruin.

THE MODERN FARM

Around the small towns and villages along the St. Lawrence where the *habitant* lives, you will see a number of prosperous and quite modern farms. Why not visit one of them? You park your car in front of a kind of big wooden cottage painted white with a pointed roof that is covered with cedar shingles. There are flowers in front of the porch, a car at the door, and a powerful tractor standing not far off. The *habitant* who owns the place comes to meet you. (In this country we say 'habitant' instead of 'paysan'.) He immediately gives you a most friendly welcome. Under his cap two blue eyes are shining in a face that is tanned by the sun and there are deep wrinkles in his cheeks and his neck. He is wearing a checked shirt with sleeves rolled up above the elbow to show a pair of hairy, muscular arms. You will hardly have time to tell your host the object of your visit before he has started to take you on a tour of his land.

The *habitant* will show you his pure-bred cattle grazing in the pasture, his big barn, his neat stable equipped with electricity and a milking machine, his great silo, and the latest in agricultural implements. Perhaps he will let you know that he won *la médaille du Mérite agricole* the year before. With a somewhat drawling accent he will explain everything in a French studded with Canadianisms and archaic expressions of considerable charm. Thus he will say 'espérez un peu' (hope a little) instead of 'attendez un peu' (wait a little), 'amarrer' (to make fast, moor) instead of 'nouer' (to knot) or 'attacher' (to tie up), and 'vache en néguère' for a cow that is dry or one that has not calved. You will listen with delight to this picturesque language, which has lost nothing of its clear syntax in spite of the vicissitudes of the centuries.

In this farmer's house you will be taken into a kind of drawing-room, neat and well furnished, but hardly ever opened except on saints' days when there are important visitors, like the curé for instance. Then when you go into other rooms, where you are taken by the *patronne* (as the wife is often called), you will notice that there is hot-air heating, a washing machine, and an electric hot-water heater along with other modern appliances. But let us hasten to underline the fact that this is a model farm, something still quite rare. There are thousands of others throughout the country where the land is less productive. There the houses and out-buildings and equipment are generally much less pretentious and the farmer who works this sometimes thankless land has to have other jobs to procure the dollar bills so urgently needed to keep things going through the dead season. Every year for seven long months the land yields nothing. You must keep in mind our winters.

THE OLD-TIME FARM

In various parts of the country there exist *habitant* families whose way of life, much less modernized, with minor exceptions resembles that of the last century. Such a farm is one of the most picturesque sights of rural Quebec.

Describing the domicile of our farmer of other days, J.-Edmond Roy wrote in his *Histoire de la Seigneurie de Lauzon*: 'The inside of the house of the French-Canadian *habitant*, lined with fir boards, is as simple as the outside. In the first room, which is used as a kitchen and bedroom, there is most important the broad open fireplace with its hearth of flat stones, the pot-hook and fire irons, the fire shovel, the big kettle and the cooking pots, saucepans and dripping-pans, baking-tins, a gridiron, another kettle, and a whole regiment of utensils, because the kitchen battery of the French-Canadian.

housewife has always been well stocked. . . . At the end of the room is the bed that belongs to the head of the house and his wife. . . . It is a veritable monument, four or five feet high with a canopy over it, and on it a pallet covered with ticking, a mattress, another mattress of feathers, with woollen blankets and sheets and pillow-slips and bolster covered with red printed cotton, then the bedspread. . . . The children's cots, folding beds or cradles, sleep in the shadow of this monumental piece of furniture.

'The rest of the furniture is scanty: five or six straw-bottomed chairs, a spinning-wheel with a reel, a frame for cloth weaving, a trough for kneading, a table and two or three chests painted over in brilliant colours. . . . In winter an iron stove burning day and night, a real hearth where they all gather, men, women, and children. There is an extraordinary confusion of everything here: preparation of food for the family and mash for the animals goes on at the same time; this is the place clothes are warmed; the ice is melted from farm implements here. . . .

Today's farm houses, even in the most back-ward areas, have been modified not only by time but also through the use of mass-produced fur-niture. Slowly and steadily they are making the transition from the land economy, from which at least ninety per cent of French Canadians come, to the industrial revolution that has taken people from the country to swell the numbers of the urban population.

In spite of everything, the *habitants* who have remained faithful to the land know that the townspeople envy them their lot in the hot summer weather. Winters have become less monotonous for them, thanks to radio and tele-vision, to the snowplough – things that enable them to maintain contact with the outside world and that enrich their thoughts and their dreams. They have even learned to have more liking for the poetic ruggedness of their winters – for the splendour of the snows whose immaculate white merges into the pure crystalline blue of a radiant sky and clothes with a magic, unreal covering the branches of pine trees and spruce, the roofs of the houses, the whole landscape as far as the eye can see.

The peoples of southern lands where the ground stays forever exposed under sun or rain cannot claim to know this planet of ours until they come and feast their eyes on such a daz-zling spectacle of white immensity.

5

Laurentian Landscapes

First there are the Laurentians north of the great river. This range of rounded mountains covered with forest stretches for hundreds of miles, from the Saguenay region in the east to the Ottawa valley in the west.

You can only realize the full splendour of these mountains from the air, when you can see for hundreds of miles. There is an incredible constellation of lakes – hundreds of thousands of them – pools, rivers, waterfalls, and rapids that stand out in contrast to the soft green of the trees.

AS THE CROW FLIES

From the air you can see the land rising and falling beneath the endless forest that varies in colour with the mixture of coniferous and deciduous trees; every hollow, every ravine reveals a flashing pool of blue in hollows of rock or sand. Here and there a fisherman's shanty or a few wooden cabins add a human note to the wilderness.

This bird's-eye view makes you want to come down to these splendid Laurentians, to sit at the foot of a white birch on the shore of a lake. Here and there trout leap at a passing fly that the swallows also chase as they skim the water with their wings; full-grown ducks, surrounded by their young, sail along the shores of the small inlets. Further on, there are in all probability summer cottages and a colony of holiday visitors in bathing suits playing on the beach or swimming and water-skiing.

This mountain region is the favourite holiday area of all Quebeckers. North of the cities especially, thousands of summer and winter cottages have sprung up around the lakes and rivers. Every week in the fine weather Montreal alone sends forth perhaps two hundred thousand of its residents into this region of matchless natural beauty, and a proportionate number go north from Quebec City.

And so from time immemorial the people of *la belle province* have had a passion for the vast open spaces, for freedom of movement, for adventure. Having crossed the Laurentians they have spread out into the magnificent region of La Tuque and Lake St. John, a sort of inland sea around which Canadian animal life abounds. And further north still they are invading the great Chibougamau territory that was opened a few years ago to prospectors and anglers. Thus in modern fashion the traditions of the *coureurs de bois* are being perpetuated.

NORTH SHORE

But the two shores of the St. Lawrence are still popular. The Charlevoix-Saguenay slopes and the Gaspé coast exert an attraction that is irresistible to anyone who knows them. It takes about an hour by car from Quebec City, travelling east along the north shore, to reach the heights of Baie Saint-Paul. From there you have a rare panoramic view. The river stretches out in sparkling waves over a breadth of twenty miles where it is almost lost in the misty blue of the south shore. It has already mingled its waters with the sea and the breeze brings you the salty tang of seaweed although you are still a long way from the ocean. Nearer to you the green mass of the Ile-aux-Coudres topped by a church steeple seems to be ploughing the St. Lawrence. It is like a canvas torn from the coast by some inspired painter. A commemorative plaque set there by the National Historic Sites and Monuments Commission states that, after anchoring his three ships, Jacques Cartier, on the sixth of September in 1535, landed on this island to which he gave its present name and the next day he attended the first mass ever said inland in this country. It is a moving page of history in a wonderful setting: below you is the little town of Baie Saint-Paul

with its houses lying in a row in the deep valley on the shores of the Rivière du Gouffre, where once there was an abundance of Atlantic salmon. A range of mountains frames the whole picture.

Continuing down river from here, Les Eboulements, Pointe-au-Pic, Cap-à-l'Aigle, Tadoussac, to name only a few, are like many jewels inlaid in the steep slopes of the Laurentian hills that plunge straight down into the river. The French way of life has perhaps been better preserved here than anywhere else, and the language as spoken there has a particular relish, with its striking images and pleasant archaisms. This is one of the favourite parts of the country for travellers and tourists. They usually take advantage of their stay in Charlevoix to make a boat trip on the Saguenay, one of the deepest rivers in the world. They go as far as Chicoutimi, past the imposing mass of capes Eternité and Trinité.

SOUTH SHORE — THE GASPÉ

The traveller at this point is only at the beginning of the delights in store. The south shore is calling now. On we go to the Gaspé.

Starting out on the south shore of the St. Lawrence from the magnificent Jacques Cartier bridge at Montreal, you may observe old French-Canadian architecture in towns and villages dating from the French régime: Boucherville, Varennes, Verchères, Contrecoeur, St-Antoine-de-Tilly, and others. In contrast to the cherished heritage there are many clusters of modern cottages and chalets built by well-to-do city-dwellers as summer homes. This is the realm of fine, tall trees – elms, maples, and giant evergreens that grow on either side of the highway.

But it is east of Quebec City that nature recaptures its grandeur. If you are not a maniac for speed you will readily stop to feel the charm of Port-Joli, so gracefully named; of Kamouraska and its islands, which are veritable bird sanctuaries; of the cape of Rivière-du-Loup, rendezvous of citizens of Quebec; of Trois-Pistoles and the cape Rioux, bristling with pines, and Ile-aux-Basques, where it is believed that Europeans landed well before the voyages of Cartier; of the incomparable Bic, with its rounded rocks that look like apocalyptic beasts floating in the St. Lawrence; of the lovely beach of Sainte-Luce; and of any number of places to beguile anyone with the soul of an artist.

The vast Gaspé peninsula lying along the Laurentian estuary is the favourite gathering-place of painters, poets, radio and television

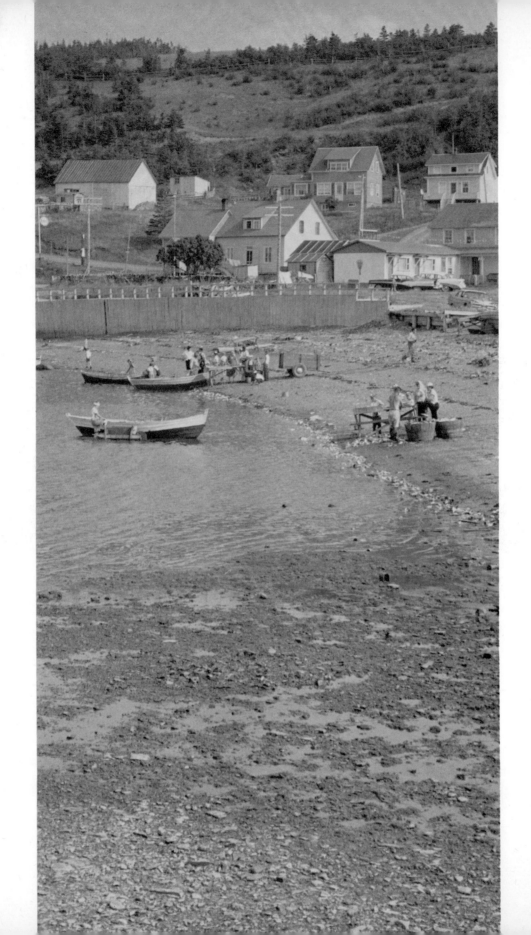

actors, theatre people, and anybody at all in love with the brilliant beauty of the seacoast.

A friend of mine who often spent his annual vacation in this marvellous spot used to say: 'When you really know the Gaspé, when you have it in your blood, you are sorry that our summers are so short and our winters so long, for you would like to be able to put up your tent and stay there forever.' The coast with its lofty rocks plunging precipitously into waves of an unreal green; the arched rocks from which the church steeple rises in the midst of simple rustic houses; the fishermen's boats rocking alongside the docks; white sails gleaming on the horizon; the lighthouses sending their pencils of light out over the dark sea – everything here has an engaging and rugged charm. All the way from Cap-Chat to Gaspé there is a series of pretty little villages where you would be happy to stay for a long time, villages like Sainte-Anne, Marsouin, and Rivière-aux-Renards, which lead to that wonder of wonders that is called Percé.

THE ENCHANTMENT OF PERCÉ

A beautiful point sculptured in stone in clear strong lines by a sea of limpid blue; a little port closed to the high winds, protected from storms

by a rock like a monstrous ship anchored in the deep. It is pierced (*percé*) in its centre where the sea passes through, and cut off at its very end to leave a kind of eternal megalithic monument pointing to heaven. Seeing it you have a feeling of being transported to some land of legend.

It is difficult to leave Percé once you begin to know its charm. You might make friends with some of the most original artists in Quebec, who would invite you to go with them to neighbouring beaches to look for the beautiful Gaspé agate.

There, just as everywhere else in the Gaspé peninsula, you will come to know the fishermen. They will welcome you with a smile, for they are very hospitable. And the sea offers a rich harvest. Cod, halibut, haddock, mackerel, lobster, herring, and other kinds of fish in great demand, have been plentiful here from time immemorial and help to feed millions of people.

THE GASPÉ FISHERMEN

There is nothing to keep you from going out to sea some fine morning in a fisherman's boat. These men are happy to anchor in a favoured place some distance out to give you the satisfaction of pulling big fish up out of the deep sea all by yourself.

When evening comes the boat returns to shore with its precious cargo. Somewhat stiff, your face sunburned, your eyes red from looking at the sunlit sea, you will be satisfied with your day.

Stepping ashore you find yourself in a forest of wide nets stretched out to dry in the sun, waiting for the next fishing. Near by are the vast racks where countless codfish, already cleaned and salted, are exposed for drying in the open air so that they will be ready for shipment to various world markets. It was with good reason that Europeans, in days gone by, used to call cod the poor man's beef. Trade in this fish that is so universally in demand has for a long time been one of the principal sources of revenue of the Gaspé peninsula.

A BIRD SANCTUARY

As a spectacle few things can be more exciting than a visit to Bonaventure Island, one of the most remarkable bird sanctuaries in America. If you go by boat along the perpendicular rock that rises high above the water you will experience the illusion of being present at a full-dress

74

aerial display. As if to greet you a host of diving waterbirds fill the air with piercing cries and the beating of wings. Gannets, cormorants, sea-gulls, sea-pigeons, grebe, and ducks of every kind fly, glide, skim over the water, dive and take a bath in the waves. Other birds by the thousands are perched on the whole immense rock that rises in front of you or lined up in the clefts, the hollows, the ledges, making it like an ever-moving coloured lacework decorating the apron of the sea.

On the vast stage of the Gaspé, Percé offers you an inspired play. In this whole peninsula, in the south as well as in the north, there are any number of glorious sites and charming fishing villages where you would be happy to stay for days and days.

6

There is a great variety of humanity in the Province of Quebec. Obviously people of French origin are to be found everywhere since they constitute the overwhelming majority; but this country is cosmopolitan in many ways that make it all the more attractive and give it character.

The ethnic make-up of Montreal, for instance, is hardly different from that of any other large Western city. People of Slav, Germanic, Mediterranean, Scandinavian, and Semitic descent rub shoulders every day with Canadians of French and English stock. At certain hours of the day as you take a walk in the business section you will catch words of ten or more languages, even Chinese.

RACIAL DIVERSITY

This racial diversity has contributed to making Montreal one of the gastronomic centres of North America, for the immigrants and their descendants have added to the native cuisine the best dishes of the different countries of Europe and Asia.

French Canadians, who are numerically dominant, are far from being a physically homogeneous type; in this there is a resemblance to

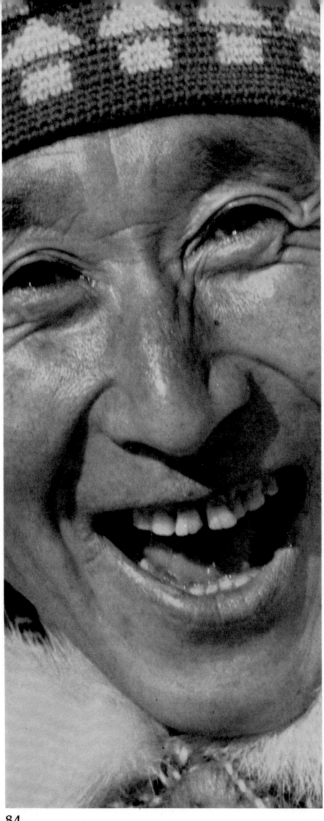

84

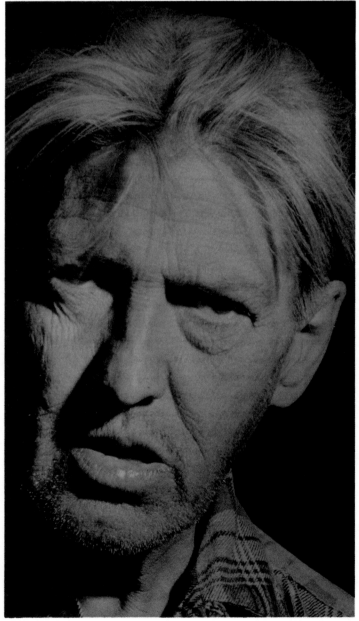

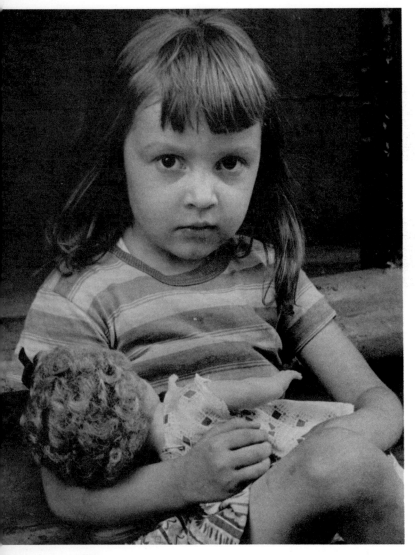

northern France. There is a complete cross-section of brunettes, blondes, and red-heads, with eyes that may be blue, light brown, dark brown, or green, and skin of every shade from lily-white to café au lait.

The descendants of the native tribes whom Cartier met on the shore of the St. Lawrence hardly exist any more, and have generally lost their special characteristics. Of those who were once called savages and who are commonly known under the name of American Indians, only a small number still live under a kind of state guardianship in reserves, and even there they have adopted our manner of living. Most of them, having lost the use of their own language, generally speak English or French. Visitors from abroad who get off the ship here expecting to see Hurons marching past under waving eagle-feathers or Iroquois dancing wildly around a fire will be greatly disappointed.

In Canada there is practically no pure-blooded race except the Eskimo of the Arctic regions. Doubtless a distant relative of the Asian peoples, whom he resembles, he still for the most part lives in his kingdom of snow and ice in the far north of Quebec where he hunts and fishes — seal, caribou, and whale — and where he builds igloos for the winter to keep out the cold.

Everywhere else Western civilization reigns. The wrinkled old farmer, smoking his pipe on his doorstep, is hardly any different from his aged cousin in Normandy. Students of both sexes, coming out through the doors of the universities of Montreal and Quebec after lectures in law, medicine, engineering, science, the humanities, and the arts, are like those in cities in the Old World, doubtless nourishing the same ambitions, with the same thoughts, the same dreams, and perhaps also the same rebellion against the past.

Here, as elsewhere, our youth has its lovers of the Bohemian life, its peculiar existentialists, and its fashionably bearded beatniks. In these groups who profess to be original there are some who are truly studious and some who have just jumped on the bandwagon. Painters make a beginning here, young musicians lose themselves in modern compositions, and budding actors wait for their opportunity.

A STRONG RACE

In this diversified society, where there is a continuation of the European culture, the features, cast of countenance, and physical characteristics

89

reveal a strong, handsome race.

The very existence of this race after so many vicissitudes of history interests and attracts the outside world. The French sensitivity is quickly discernible: the people are lively, spontaneous, responsive. Faces come to life more quickly than elsewhere. Words of happiness or anger burst out more explosively. That passionate feelings betray themselves so readily in the face of a French Canadian is in contrast to the way of an Anglo-Saxon, whose emotions boil behind a façade of enforced calm and conventions.

All these outward manifestations of feelings find spoken expression in French. In the middle class, where education and family upbringing have corrected the rough spots in the speech of farmer or woodsman, except in accent the language is no different from that spoken in France. Many Frenchmen landing in Quebec for the first time feel they are still at home.

Much more vivid, more picturesque, is the language of the farmer or the fisherman, and especially of the man with the weather-beaten face who works as a woodsman. His vigorous speech, studded with phrases that he rolls on his tongue with relish, is in the process of disappearing. But I hope that you may still have a

chance to hear it, perhaps from the lips of an old guide as he is taking you into the heart of the forest in French Canada.

7

Around the Traditional Hearth

Throughout the long summer when you drive along the Quebec highways, as you enter or leave the villages you will often see strange colourful displays of materials and objects brightly decorating windows. If you are curious you will not be able to resist stopping at least once. And you will not be sorry because you will be making the acquaintance of French-Canadian handicraft.

In most cases the articles exhibited in these places have been manufactured in typical homes of our country people during the long winter months. Woollen blankets with splashes of blue or red or pink, braided or hooked rugs, linen tablecloths or table napkins, belts woven in an arrow pattern (*ceintures fléchées*), lying beside factory-made knick-knacks that are in sharp contrast to the handmade things.

The rural population of Quebec has in no way lost the tradition of another time when every hearth, transformed into a workshop, was able to provide everything the family needed. There they carded, spun, and warped wool and even flax for linen; there they made clothes and bedsheets from materials woven by experienced hands; there they braided straw hats and knitted caps and stockings and shawls. Such was the

enormous contribution of the French-Canadian woman to her home up to the end of the nineteenth century. Every woman had to have nimble fingers and incredible stamina. Meanwhile, in the midst of these many tasks, she baked bread, served meals, and raised eight, ten, or a dozen children.

The men also worked at the most varied trades. Besides being farm labourers and lumbermen, they were, as the need arose, carpenters, woodworkers, masons, butchers. They built their own houses and stables and sleighs. When autumn came they butchered pigs, young cattle, sheep, and turkeys for winter meat, for winter itself provided an immense refrigerator. Sometimes the butchering was the occasion for gargantuan feasts.

For the most part, the availability of mass-produced goods has put an end to this régime of self-sufficiency. But a good number of women have not forgotten the domestic skills practised by their grandmothers and the men have retained, at least in part, the particular ability of their forebears to undertake almost any manual work. They are still very skilful in building log cabins in our mountains and many holiday people are indebted to them for their summer cottages.

In recent times Quebec has ceased to be an agricultural and rural country. The urban population is now much the larger. But our middle class, almost all originally from the farm, the class of professional men and women as well as of businessmen, artists, and intellectuals, have inherited from that past some of the virtues of endurance and know-how that explain the French-Canadian miracle.

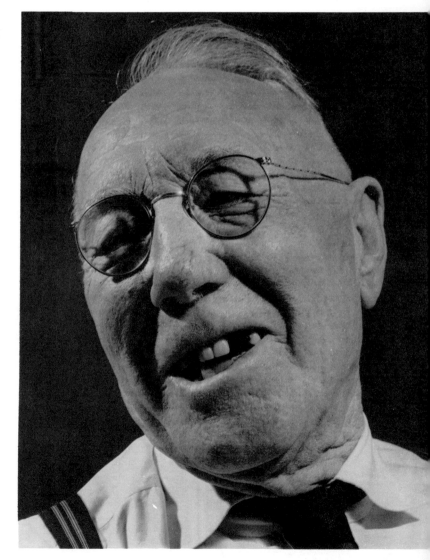

8   *Clergy and Nuns*

Religious orders and organizations are abundantly represented in Quebec, where the great majority of the French-speaking population is Roman Catholic. This is explained by the fact that New France, abandoned by its lay élite after the surrender of the country to England, could scarcely count on anybody except its clergy to organize its schools. It is generally considered that had it not been for their initiative, French language and culture in America would have ended.

Our seminaries, our large classical colleges, and our French-language universities are clerical establishments to which monks and secular priests have always furnished an incalculable number of professors in all branches of human knowledge. Only quite recently has a lay staff of some importance been brought into these institutions, where the humanities hold the place of honour and men are moulded for positions of leadership.

Following the old seminary of Quebec in the provincial capital and the college of the Sulpicians in Montreal, other institutions of classical learning soon appeared and their number continued to grow. In addition, the great monastic orders – notably the Jesuits and the Dominicans

100

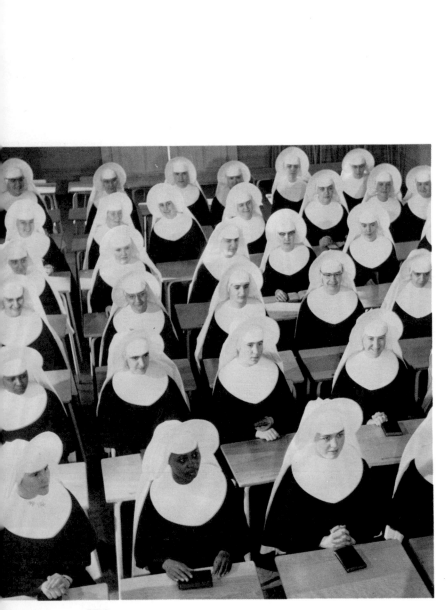

– provide cultural centres of great value.

For the education of the masses the teaching orders of brothers and nuns have covered the country with convents and large schools. In this way no locality however isolated, even deep in the bush, is totally deprived of teachers, and illiteracy is almost unknown.

RELIGION WITHOUT AUSTERITY

Some people imagine that the existence of so many seminaries, monasteries, and cloisters gives Quebec a solemn face. Possibly this was once true, but not in our time. More and more monks and nuns have been making contact with the laity and the secular world. Not only have they entered resolutely into the field of the arts and sciences, but they have established between themselves and the great family of students a close relationship that has grown out of the best kind of good fellowship. So it is that active sports are not unknown to them. Even the good sisters, in spite of their habits and monastic head-dress, play volley-ball with as much zest as their most sports-minded pupils. On their side the reverend brothers could very well give a few lessons to their pupils in football, basket-ball, baseball, tennis, and hockey. Long practice in democratic living and the necessity for adapting to modern times have brought about these closer relations without damage to the prestige of coif or cassock.

The people, for the most part, welcome the trend to contemporary ideas with more understanding today than formerly, even when the ideas seem to be in disagreement with their traditional faith. Socially they fraternize with men of every faith, without going back on their principles, however, for they remain deeply religious. They love and support their fine churches, which attract a whole multitude of men and women from different countries. From the United States alone come hundreds of thousands of pilgrims every year, anxious to see the famous sanctuaries of Sainte-Anne, Notre-Dame-du-Cap, and the Oratoire Saint-Joseph, three of the most remarkable monuments of the faith in America.

9

Poets like to give the name 'children of the gods' to the men and women who devote their lives to expressing, in the visual or plastic arts, the ideal forms of the infinitely diverse world around and within them. These children are legion in French Canada. Already some of our artists have acquired an international reputation. A beginning has been made that shows no sign of slowing down.

It seems to be in painting that Quebec up to now has become best known. Merely to cite the names of Pellan, Borduas, Riopelle, and their many colleagues is to evoke the most exciting moments of our artistic evolution.

Our schools of fine art, the scholarships abroad, especially to Paris, and the dynamic progress of several young men of exceptional talent have inspired a group of painters whose numerous exhibitions demonstrate originality and strength. Although some seem to have a limited ability, you discern others with serious promise for the future.

To anyone living in Montreal, for instance, or simply passing through, a visit to the Museum of Fine Art and to some ten first-rate galleries promises interest. And to find creative talent at work one might go to some studio or other,

perhaps set up in the country under the fine, clear light of the Canadian sky.

But there is not only painting. Out of stone, marble, bronze, wood, and clay several of our sculptors have created living forms in every style from academic realism to the most daring surrealism. Along with the artists aiming at the universal are sculptors in wood who excel in anecdote and characterization. The Bourgault brothers have made a great reputation for themselves in this genre. Figures of country men and women, silhouettes of workers on the farm or in the forest, domestic animals, saints in paradise, all come from their hands as if alive and breathing. This is how there was born, at Saint-Jean-Port-Joli, a small industry that really deserves to prosper.

Others design and make pottery and have succeeded in creating new shapes. For lack of material means and experience they are still far from producing the charming figurines of Dresden and Limoges; but in these efforts you witness the first steps to establishing enterprises in which business and art will get along together. Meanwhile a number of collectors are acquiring good pieces from our best potters and will not regret having done so.

112

Some lovers of jewels exercise their talents cutting and polishing semiprecious stones that they have picked up on the shores of the Gaspé. They make charming objects from them — pendants, earrings, rings. These pretty things are worn as so many lasting memories of summer holidays.

It is rightly said that French Canadians are a musical people. All types of classical music find outstanding interpreters. We have several composers in the best tradition. And the government has founded and supports conservatories with good teaching staffs.

It is the same for the dramatic arts. Although popular theatre is not yet well established in Quebec, even in Montreal, French-language radio and television can draw on any number of first-class actors and actresses.

But perhaps it is the *chansonette* that has shown the greatest development and the greatest success. This province already possessed the richest heritage of folklore in Canada. To this has been added hundreds of songs, some of which will one day be known around the world. Félix Leclerc's songs are sung in France as well as in Canada. Other singers like young Claude Gauthier have become known in the United

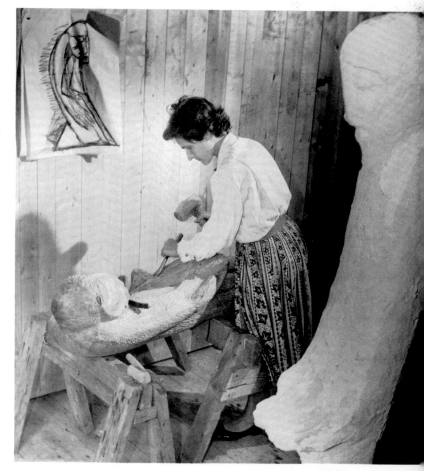

States. Latin America will not be long in giving them a welcome.

Certain religious houses are no strangers to this delight. One of the best known and most popular monks, Father de Brienne, who gives part of his leisure time to surrealist painting, composes songs that he sings to his own accompaniment on the guitar to the great delight of his listeners.

In short the artistic sense of the people shows itself in all sorts of ways and in every form of art, major or minor, and only needs the greater audience outside our borders to keep on growing.

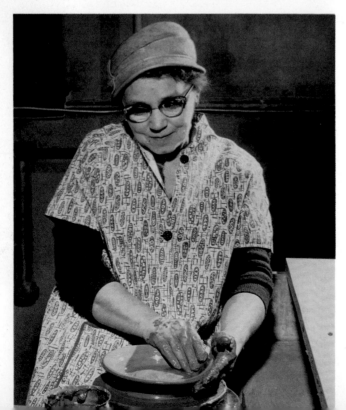

10 *Sport*

Hockey is the national sport of French Canadians. For them it is the finest sport in the world. They are probably right. Have you ever been in the huge amphitheatre of the Montreal Forum on a Saturday night? What a show!

The great arena, gleaming like a sheet of blue glass, is bathed in a dazzling light. It seems to be waiting for a company of super-stars, Wagnerian heroes determined on the conquest and possession of glory. The crowd, too, is waiting. Fifteen thousand eager spectators, quivering with breathless impatience, are crowded into the tiers of seats; fifteen thousand pairs of eyes are fixed on the gate where the players will appear at any minute. Suddenly, a tremendous shout and hand-clapping. Fifteen thousand pairs of lungs bursting in the same split second. One by one the tricoloured sweaters are silhouetted against the gleaming crystal and the steel blades bite into the ice, tracing a thousand geometric patterns. While these favourites of the crowd are performing with the elegance of ballerinas, the players of the opposing team in their turn make their appearance while the applause, though not meant for them, keeps on ringing.

117

A UNIQUE SPECTACLE

The battle is about to begin; but before it does there is a singularly moving ceremony. The two teams line up facing each other at attention. The whole crowd stands and is quiet and into the silence the orchestra launches the impressive strains of the national anthem. (Here it is always 'O Canada'.) At the last note the applause starts again and play begins. There are moments when you might say that the national honour is at stake.

In this fascinating game there is a popular tendency not unique to it: the cult of the hero. Maurice Richard, who was the most spectacular player in the National Hockey League, is the best example of this. Because of his numerous exploits in every arena in the league, he has become a kind of legend. He was known in Quebec as Mr. Hockey, and elsewhere as the Rocket. His photograph would appear in daily newspapers and on posters; he was held up to school boys and girls as someone to be admired. Every youngster learning to skate dreamed some day of being a Maurice Richard. And now that he has retired in glory the crowd is searching desperately among its young athletes for someone who will grow to the stature of the former

118

star. But with or without Richard, hockey, of which Montreal is the capital, remains the favourite sport of the crowd.

SKIING

Formerly unknown in America, skiing, imported from Europe, has rapidly gained great popularity in Quebec as in the rest of Canada. Because of our long winters, which make this sport practicable from the beginning of December to the end of March, and the hundreds of accessible slopes all along the Laurentians and in several places in the Eastern Townships, skiing can only become more popular.

Centres like Beauport north of Quebec City, or Mont-Tremblant, Saint-Adèle, Sainte-Agathe, Saint-Sauveur, and Saint-Donat north of Montreal, to name only a few of them, welcome at least a hundred thousand skiers of all ages and conditions every week-end. Mountain slopes blossom with multi-coloured sweaters, now in the blinding light of sun on snow, now in wind and light snowfall. When evening comes people scatter into the numerous hotels, cottages, or boarding-houses in the district. After a strenuous day of skiing, perhaps at ten or twenty degrees below zero, it is good to relax in front

of huge maple logs blazing in a stone fireplace. This is the hour for apéritifs, good stories, some boasting, and much innocent flirtation.

Before skis were much used, Canadians had nothing but snowshoes for winter travel in forest or field. In winter snowshoes were, for the *coureur de bois*, the lumberman, and the trapper, what the birch-bark canoe was in the summer – that is to say, a vital necessity. They

are still indispensable to the man working in the woods, to the trapper and a good many others. But snowshoeing has not been written off as a sport. Clubs still exist, organizing races every year in which the participants, dressed in checkered blue, red, green, and white with the famous arrow-patterned sash around the waist, present a most picturesque appearance.

SKATING

Canada has sent to the Olympic Games some of the best skaters in the world. In Quebec as in the rest of the country (with the exception of Southern Ontario and the Pacific Coast in British Columbia), every village, every hamlet, every town, large or small, has open-air skating rinks for four or five months of the year. Every day children and grown-ups come there in great numbers. Hardly have boys and girls started to walk when they put on skates and in a short time learn to cut figures on the glittering ice. The most talented have ambitions either for a career in hockey or to be crowned king or queen of figure-skating in world competition. In elegance this sport can compare to the ballet.

OTHER SPORTS

Every winter, bob-sleds shoot down the icy runs of the Quebec City embankment and elsewhere. There are perilous canoe races through the moving ice of the St. Lawrence, and races for the dog-sled teams which have long been used in the far north of Quebec. No winter carnival could get along without these exhibitions of skill and endurance.

In summer there are all kinds of water sports on the thousands of lakes and rivers of this countryside. Swimming, sailing, yachting, water-skiing, and skin-diving are all enthusiastically pursued by the young people.

This picture would be incomplete without mention of the increasingly popular bicycle races. To be sure Quebec has nothing to compare to the Tour de France which arouses an interest over there comparable to the World Series in the United States; but the Quebec-Montreal race inaugurated a few years ago is still growing in popularity. We may see the day when our province, because of its immense size, creates a Tour de Québec that will be the envy even of the former mother country.

11

Quebec, land of the future. It is in these words that one has to characterize this province that is three times the size of France and has scarcely five million inhabitants. No region of North America offers a more promising future. Its wealth has scarcely been touched. But a nation at work is beginning to reveal these riches to the world.

WEALTH FROM THE TREE

Forests, waterfalls, and mines of all kinds, which are already playing such an important role in the economy of French Canada, will make it one of the wealthy areas of the continent.

The forests that are the beauty of this country are its wealth as well. They cover an immense territory. The stranger coming here for the first time is filled with astonishment and admiration when he sees them. Everywhere his eye feeds on the sight of the beautiful trees, even in towns as populous as Montreal. Let him travel over our countryside and he will go along roads lined with leafy trees and evergreens.

Many different varieties of tree produce wood suitable for construction of furniture – maple, silver and white birch, pine, fir, ash, cedar, and poplar, not to mention the many species of fruit trees.

But it is the cone-bearing and resin-producing trees, the spruce and the fir, that now and for some time past have brought the biggest profits. In the forests have risen great mills to manufacture pulp and paper which we export to various countries, especially to the United States. From them we derive a profit of hundreds of millions of dollars, and this industry employs thousands of workmen.

In the winter gangs of lumbermen invade our forests. The trees that they fell methodically over large areas are hauled to rivers or lakes to await the spring drive. In the past the cutting was done with the axe. Here as elsewhere mechanization has been introduced, making the work faster and easier. The power-saw has taken the place of the cross-cut saw and motor vehicles have supplanted the horses. Bulldozers cut roads for trucks to transport logs, and the winter countryside is thus opened up to the outside world.

Lumbermen are rough fellows who love their work and who nowadays make a lot of money. The lumber camps, where they are lodged and fed, are comfortable. The old sense of isolation

129

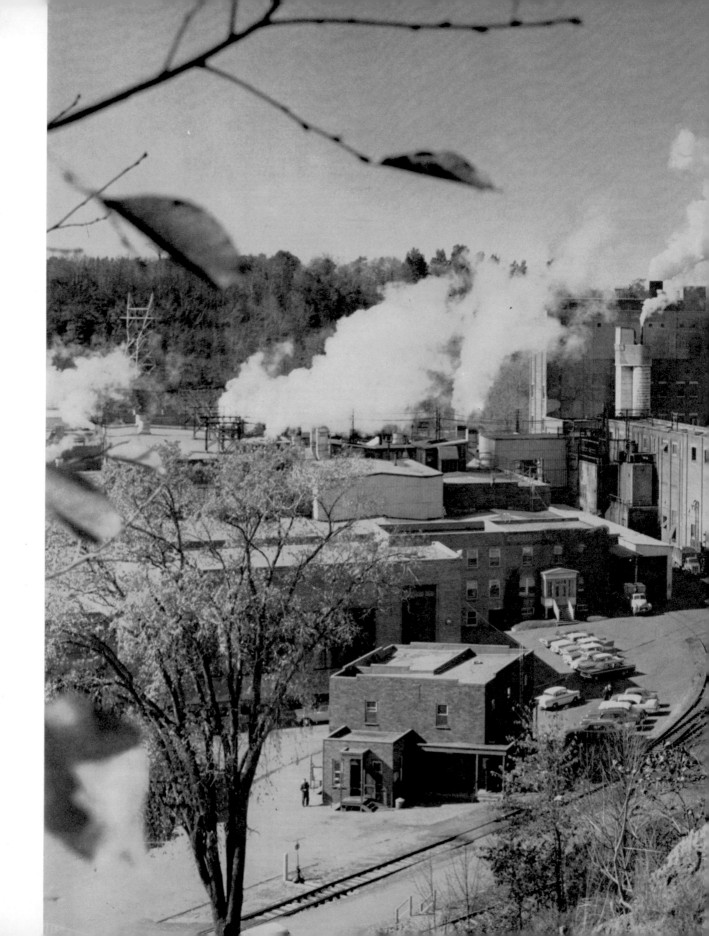

and captivity in the wilderness has disappeared with the advent of radio and television. A gasoline motor and a generator provide the whole establishment with electricity. The lumberman now has plenty of light to read by or to gaze at the pin-up girl at the head of his bed.

These camps are well worth visiting if only to enjoy a substantial meal after a long day's trip through the snowy forests. For few workers are as well fed as these robust men – hearty eaters, all of them famished, who might rough up the cook should he blunder and not have enough steak or roast beef or pork and beans or serve poorly baked pie. Lumbermen have the reputation of being hard to please when it comes to food.

THE DRIVE

The drive – known here as *la drave* from the English word – is a dangerous and picturesque lumbering operation. Nearly the whole winter's harvest of logs is carried to the pulp-and-paper mills on the streams that rush from heights toward the river and the sea. With the help of

133

the spring floods, controlled by temporary dams, the trees, cut into four-foot logs, are steered by the million towards their destination many miles away. Gangs of loggers follow them on foot along the whole length of the journey, overseeing from the steep slopes and scrub of the river banks this forest on the move. There is nothing more thrilling than the sight of the logs descending the rapids, the sound of the rushing water, heavy and ice-cold, a sound that is the herald of summer, the log jams in the falls or the foam along the shallows, the stream driven back in eddies of white froth, the log jams being broken up by exploding charges of dynamite, the bare trunks rolling over each other, standing on end, then falling back and starting off again as if in panic.

This is the first step in the publication of the majority of the great newspapers the world over. Each of us when reading current events and commentaries should sometimes stop and think that the frail sheet of paper that he holds in his hands is the result of marvellous transformations. Once it was a tree on the shores of a river, born to give a nesting-place to birds, shade to wild beasts, and a refuge to partridge pursued by the fox. When it grew high and strong and

handsome it felt the steel saw cut into its trunk near the root and began the long pilgrimage. Men cut off its branches, sliced it into logs, then floated it over the swollen spring streams to the mill to grind it to pulp and press it into immense rolls of newsprint, paper that will carry truth and lies, the stories of countless human dramas – news.

HOME OF ELECTRICITY

Quebec is one of the few lands where there is no coal-mining. On the other hand it has an extraordinary supply of water-power. Considering its population and industrial development, it is already the biggest producer of electricity in the world and in this field its unexploited resources are immense. The fresh-water lakes and streams that are in such abundance are the beauty of this territory and its wealth as well. Our economic future in great part depends on this, considering that the huge volume of cheap power is bound to attract new industries and create new towns.

No one can pride himself on really knowing Quebec if he has not seen some of the places that our electric power comes from. You feel the overwhelming energy of our rapids, of our

roaring falls, of our huge dams, of our vast water reservoirs and our superb power-houses that distribute power and life to town and country. On the heights of the St. Maurice or the Gatineau, in the Lake St. John basin where the marvellous Saguenay has its source, or at different points on the North Shore you will find important hydro-electric plants to admire as you travel through some of the most attractive country in North America. You will realize then the importance of what the Quebec government acquired when it nationalized electricity in 1963.

UNDERGROUND RESOURCES

The underground wealth of Quebec has been scarcely tapped. According to geologists this region will become sooner or later one of the principal producers of all kinds of metals and minerals in the world. In different spots in the province mining centres of interest already exist. The Abitibi copper and gold mines, like the asbestos mines at Thetford Mines in the Eastern Townships, are well known. The so-called barren lands of Chibougamau north of Lake St. John are rich with promise. Further on, much further, right to the Arctic, in areas until now known only to the Eskimoes, the trappers, and

the herds of caribou, the bleak tundra and even those endless stretches covered with ice certainly hide unsuspected treasures.

Take Ungava, for example, the area that stretches from the North Shore of the St. Lawrence to fade off into the frigid seas. This space, which would hold the whole of France, used to be called 'the land God gave to Cain' because in its barrenness, its silence, and its air of solitude it is the image of despair. And now the land of Cain has become the land of the future. Deposits of iron that are among the most important on the continent were discovered here a few years ago and work on them has begun since then. Hundreds of millions of tons of this precious metal will be taken out and sent to various North American steel mills. The day is quickly coming when the ore will be smelted and transformed into finished products here in Quebec for export to the world.

Thanks to these developments on the North Shore, where there used to be only a few outposts of civilization and where the principal attraction consisted of salmon streams – a paradise for millionaire Canadians or Americans – there are now prosperous new towns along the river. An improved road connects these centres

141

with Montreal and Quebec going by way of
La Malbaie, the Saguenay River, and Tadoussac;
bridges span the streams, and a new railway
reaches far into the interior. So a second Gaspé,
wilder than the other, appears for men to
explore and admire.

CHARCOAL

Making charcoal is a small local industry that
cannot be compared in importance to heavy
industry. It is, however, probably more charac-
teristic because it is more representative of
this country, whose forests run far beyond the
little areas cleared by men.

The charcoal ovens, lined up over a vast area,
resemble huge bee-hives in shape. Near by you

142

144

see heaps of logs waiting for the 'baking' that will transform them into a fuel indispensable to certain industries and widely used in a great number of Canadian fireplaces.

The manpower, recruited especially among the farmers, is made up of eager, interesting fellows who will be only too glad to explain the process of manufacturing a kind of coal that does not require them to work a thousand feet underground as the coal miners do.

145

Of course the preceding picture shows only a few aspects of the Quebec economy. This has been developing at increasing speed in the last few years. It includes almost all the industrial and commercial activities of any progressive North American region.

148

12

Maple Sugar

The maple leaf is a national emblem. It is on our flag, and with good reason. Aside from its value as a fine wood widely used in the furniture and building industries, the maple is the glory of our autumn and the joy of our spring. It grows almost everywhere, in the depths of the distant evergreen forest or nearer to hand, and it reaches giant proportions.

In the last days of September or early in October all of Quebec is decked in improbably gay and splendid colours. Every part of the country – the north and south shores of the great river, Beauce, the Eastern Townships, the Laurentians, La Tuque, the Gaspé, the Ottawa valley – is covered over as if with huge flowers, in reds and yellows and light browns and gold. All these shades are so brilliant that they look like a display of fireworks extending to infinity. Our mountains are clothed and set on fire with them, from the peaks to the floor of the valleys. We owe this spectacular colour, the despair of painters, particularly to the maple leaves in autumn. At the moment when they are about to fall from the branch under the relentless north wind, the maple leaves cover the tree with a cloak of the orient as if they were defying oblivion, as if they were trying to people our

149

winter dreams with fantastic visions.

The other way this stately tree invades the thoughts of man is through the taste of the sap that streams up to all its branches with the first spring thaws, about the end of March or beginning of April. There are no wild-flowers or green grass before the middle of May, and deep snow shrouds the undergrowth. But the sun, growing strong now, shines on the frozen tree trunks, and the liquid sap is already beginning to turn the world green again. 'Sap's running!' The words will ring out in hundreds of country homes some evening: 'Sap's running!' The children clap their hands when they hear it; they listen ecstatically to their father saying, 'To-morrow morning, Pierre, you will hitch up the mare to the big sleigh and take the clean barrel along to the maple grove. We're going to tap the trees.' This means that they will drill holes with brace and bit in the trunk of every maple tree in the grove, fitting in metal spouts through which the sap will flow drop by drop into aluminum buckets.

The precious liquid that is gathered and poured into the barrel twice a day – depending on the weather – will be transformed in a few

152

hours into a syrup that gourmets dote on.

There is a sugaring hut in the maple grove, a humble affair made of boards and divided into two parts. One part, furnished with a large table and rustic benches, is kept for the family and guests or visitors; the other contains the big heating-kettle where the filtered maple sap, cleaned of impurities, is briskly boiled down. The liquid as it thickens becomes, successively, the *trempette*, a clear, very sweet liquid that is delicious eaten on bread; the syrup, amber-coloured, which has a taste that is infinitely more pleasant and more delicate than cane syrup; then the *tire*, the taffy, that is spread in thin slabs on snow and eaten right away, as much of it as possible, although it can be kept for several days; finally the fragrant golden sugar, shaped into blocks that weigh from two to four pounds or into figures of people and animals to delight small children.

In the hours when the sap is boiling down, the hut is saturated with the exquisite maple aroma. Visitors from town love this aroma which is a great stimulant for the appetite. Every week-end when the weather is fine they invade our maple groves in organized groups. It is *la fête aux sucres*.

There is dancing, singing, eating, and drinking.
Nearly all of French-Canadian folklore is there.
Before the party ends the notes of 'Alouette,
gentille alouette' burst into the steamy air of the
hut where everybody is having the time of his
life. But the maple syrup does not serve simply
as pretext for a party. Far from it. For three
centuries it has helped to feed the family. More
than that, thanks to improved methods of
manufacture, it has conquered a considerable
part of the North American market.

Syrup is by far the most popular of all maple
products today, but old-fashioned maple sugar
remains a favourite in many Canadian homes.
On our tables it recalls a time when the pioneers
used to collect the sap in wooden troughs and
boil it down to sugar in enormous iron kettles.
For many of us it was the dessert we liked best
year-round. It is found in a number of recipes
that do credit to the Canadian cuisine.

155

13

Fishing as a Sport

Fresh-water salmon fishing is a royal sport available especially to rich men or poachers. An American fisherman used to estimate the cost of one twenty-pound fish caught in Canada at three hundred dollars. Nearly all the rivers where this vigorous fish comes up to spawn every year after a long sojourn at sea have been farmed out to clubs whose members have to have the money to allow them the luxury. Dues, tackle, guides, travel costs, board, alcohol, everything is expensive. But for anyone who has the means, the reward is worth the expense.

TO GO SALMON FISHING

The areas where the salmon abound are far removed from the big centres. Nearly all of them are on the North Shore between Tadoussac and Labrador, in the Gaspé peninsula, and in the tributaries of the St. Lawrence and Chaleur Bay. Other species of salmon that live in land-locked lakes and consequently never go to the sea are fished in a few places and are not lacking in interest. There are some in Lake Magog and in Lake St. John, known as *ouananiches*. They are less appreciated than their brothers the sea-going salmon.

Fly-fishing is the method used to fish for

159

salmon: that is to say, casting with bright-coloured bait. One day when I was the poor guest of a rich friend I happened to hook a salmon that weighed more than thirty pounds. It was an indescribable sensation. From the canoe, I struggled with the monster for more than an hour. After a series of leaps and tricks of every kind he dragged me into the rapids along with my two guides, who had to exert extreme care to keep the canoe from the rocks and avoid sudden movements, until at last the salmon, exhausted but still in fighting mood, succumbed to the gaff. There is nothing more exciting, believe me.

SPECKLED TROUT

In this country anybody who has never fished for speckled trout at least once in his life is looked upon as something of a nature-hater. Every summer at least half a million Que-beckers, men, women, and children, indulge in this sport that leaves one of their happiest of holiday memories.

The speckled or brook trout is very hand-some. Its body, covered with flourishes of brown and gold with a play of blue or silver, is marked over its whole length with little spots of vivid

162

red. It is found nearly everywhere in Canada and in the American states along the border. In Quebec it is found in all regions from the tributaries of the Arctic to the southern Eastern Townships. Attempts to transplant the speckled trout to Europe have been unsuccessful.

Like the salmon, this hardy fish (maximum weight of five to six pounds, but averaging one-half to two pounds for those caught) is usually fished with the fly. The angler would feel him-self disgraced if he used a worm as bait; he leaves this method to the people he contemptu-ously refers to as *carpons*.

The best fishing-grounds for these *moucheurs*, as they are called, are the Gaspé peninsula, the Charlevoix-Saguenay shore, the La Tuque region, lakes St. John and Chibougamau, all of the region north of Quebec City including the well-stocked Parc des Laurentides, the St. Mau-rice highlands, the numerous club reserves in the west Laurentian sector in which Tremblant is situated, and a number of lakes and rivers in the Eastern Townships. Unfortunately waters that could provide good fishing have been com-pletely ruined because they were left open to the public too long without adequate super-vision, especially near the towns. From this

point of view the ease of motor travel has been disastrous. But enough good areas are left to satisfy the most enthusiastic and the most particular fishermen.

At the age of ten or eleven I was already learning the art of fly-fishing. This was in my beautiful Charlevoix country. The icy mountain water, first filtered among moss, pine trunks,

and greenish rocks, and then joining countless clear brooks, creates those rivers with their little white waterfalls and dark eddies where the trout, liking the cold clear and the shade, circles and plays and multiplies. In bare feet, barking my shins on the needle-sharp thorns of the raspberry bushes, tearing my pants on the protruding dry branches, I would make my way down to the bottom of the ravines where the stream sings its monotone song. And there, walking right out into the river, leaping from rock to rock, sometimes tripping and falling flat on my face, I would fish madly until evening when I would bring home a good string of small trout.

A TYPICAL FISHING TRIP

Since then I have taken my fishing tackle over the whole Laurentian paradise. From the countless memories, let me single out one in particular because it will recall similar stories to any ardent fisherman. It was north of Saint-Raymond near Quebec City. For seven whole days we lived on the shores of an enchanted lake, sleeping in a tent on fragrant fir boughs. The squirrels woke us before dawn, squealing and playing hide-and-seek over our heads; hares poked their noses in at our door and a chubby ground-hog

165

would walk about on the log table that we had set up beside the tent. In the evening the blue smoke of an improvised cook-stove would filter up through the branches of the spruce and tamarack while the smell of fish being fried in butter gave an edge to our appetite.

My companions and I had kept, to take back to town and impress our friends, about sixty fine fish of two to three pounds. At the end of the last day we were fishing very late, by moonlight. Then, throwing my line into the brook near its mouth, I felt something on it that was so powerful, so heavy, that the guide, noticing how my fishing rod was bent, gave a joyous shout: 'Why, it's a damned ox!' For twenty minutes I had to struggle with this ox while it refused to give in. It weighed five pounds. It was the prize of the trip. To get to that place we had driven up twelve miles of mountain road and crossed bad pontoon bridges in a small truck that jounced and creaked and threatened broken bones; then we had portaged seven miles over a bumpy path, carrying heavy packs on our backs while hungry mosquitoes swarmed around our heads.

At the end of the trip, dirty, bearded, with forehead, ears, and neck studded with insect

168

bites, but refreshed in soul and body, we went home to civilization with the picture well fixed in our minds of a beautiful blue lake where birches are mirrored in the water, where loons cry and where the great moose bathe. When cold and snow come we shall relive these scenes and we shall have a mighty longing for the virgin forest.

OTHER GOOD FISHING

Other interesting kinds of fish claim the attention of the fisherman who loves the sport. Grey trout and lake trout – two varieties of the same family – are large fish weighing from fifteen to twenty pounds and more when full grown. These are caught by trolling with a glittering lure. They offer a fierce resistance to anybody hooking them. The muskellunge is fished in the same way in the deep waters of the St. Lawrence. It is voracious, powerful, and pugnacious. When it is hungry it will bite at anything. Fish of twenty pounds and more are fairly common. There is an abundance, too, of pike and seabream (dorado) in many places and they are considered good fishing.

But much to be preferred by the fisherman who casts is the indefatigable bass. In proportion to its weight – not more than a few pounds – it puts up an even more savage resistance than salmon or trout.

For people who live in warm climates and who are unacquainted with our winters and their phenomena, nothing will appear as peculiar, as incredible, as the spectacle of people fishing through holes cut in the ice for tomcod (smelt). From a foot to three feet thick depending on how cold it is, the ice serves as flooring and foundation for hundreds of huts set up on Lac Saint-Pierre, a broadening of the St. Lawrence River upstream from Three Rivers. Every winter you see a veritable village rising on a huge expanse of ice, in the very spot where great ships pass from March to December. People live there, eat, drink, and keep warm, protected from any wind, in temperatures from fifteen to thirty degrees below zero while they bring to the icy surface ton after ton of tomcod. In spite of such a massacre this fish is indestructible – a good thing, because it is delicious. It has come from the salt-water zone of the great river, that is to say from a very long distance, to lay its innumerable eggs in fresh water on the sandy bottom of Lac Saint-Pierre. People can go on catching them forever and there will still be enough for the gourmets and for the thousands of people fascinated by the old sport that combines snow and ice and water.

14

Anyone who has the good fortune to spend the summer in one of our forests an hour or two away from our big cities will not fail to see strange visitors around his cottage. Fine specimens of Canadian animals will come by, especially if he is living on the shore of a lake.

From the windows of a property in the Laurentians that I have been going to for more than twenty years, I have seen deer, beavers, otters, muskrats, mink, porcupine, and, of course, hares in abundance. Entire families of partridge have walked among our blueberries while all kinds of songbirds flew about in our trees and loons and various kinds of ducks disported themselves on the lake. Because Quebec is a country of mountains and forests and lakes and streams, and because the climate is propitious, its fauna is one of the most diversified in the world.

KING OF THE FOREST

The largest of the deer family, the moose or American elk, has found its favourite habitat in our land. This splendid beast, with the stature of a horse and enormous antlers spreading in double-fan shape over a span of three to four feet, haunts the dreams of all big-game hunters.

He is one of nature's wonders.

When he does not feel in danger of being fired on, the moose shows a tendency to want to be near man. Some have been known to spend whole seasons among herds of cattle or where horses are pastured. The story is told, for instance, of a farmer who, after succeeding in taming one of them to the point of shutting him up in a barn, had all kinds of trouble later on in getting rid of his cumbersome guest. On the lake where we have our summer home a young female spent the months of August and September 1960 among the people vacationing there. Every day she would stand on the shore to watch the passing canoes, rowboats, and motorboats, and the people in them would call out and wave to her. You would have said that it interested her. She let anybody who wanted take pictures of her. She even took it calmly when one photographer went so far as to pat her on the nose – and that before my very eyes after I had beached my boat right at her feet. She disappeared at last in mating time. Only love could take her away from us.

It is the same thing in the national parks where hunting is strictly prohibited. This picturesque animal, knowing that he is safe, does

not even take the trouble to get out of the way of cars. He has been known to block the road and cause serious accidents. One can only be sorry for the drivers who take foolish risks.

But wherever he knows he is being tracked the moose is on the look-out and is not easily taken unawares. He then demonstrates that he can be as cunning as man. He senses man's presence from a long way off and makes incredible detours to outwit him. If surprised, he flees with the speed of a train and you wonder by what miracle his great antlers do not slow him up as he makes his way through dense thickets at that speed.

The improved weapons of today and the growing army of hunters would mean the end of this enormous target for hunters, were it not for government preserves and game laws. Only such safeguards can save the moose from extinction.

The poacher, the wolf, and even the aeroplane are perhaps the worst enemies of moose. The herd spends the winter imprisoned in the restricted space of its grounds and can't get out until spring. Not only does it become the prey of wolves at this time but it can easily be spotted by plane and massacred by individuals who

know neither law nor pity. These poachers go by snowshoe to the grounds spotted from the air, kill several defenceless animals, cut off the hind-quarters, which make excellent steaks, and leave the rest of the carcass on the snow. Every year police arrest some of these destroyers; but it is hoped that intelligent educational campaigns will in time end the carnage.

Relentless war is being waged against wolves. Rifle and poison have destroyed countless of these prolific and cunning animals, but many survive. However, in attacking wolves we must consider that they are less dangerous to moose than man is, and they have the excuse that they must hunt to survive.

THE BLACK BEAR

A few years ago, black bears used to visit our summer place in the Laurentians every year. A she-bear and her young ones once came up on our kitchen verandah, doubtless in the hope of finding something good to eat. She left silently without causing any damage. The ferocity of this peaceful animal has been greatly exaggerated. It asks nothing better than to remain hidden and so avoid meeting man, whose power it knows. Only the female, when she

174

thinks her little ones are in danger, will become aggressive and capable of anything, even murder, to protect her young.

Meeting a bear on one of your forest meanderings must not frighten you too much. In national parks where there is no shooting it gets familiar to the point of coming to eat at your feet, sometimes even out of your hands. But do not touch it. A slap from its paw is dangerous even when it has no intention of doing you any harm. It simply does not know its own strength.

To protect their sheep, farmers have thought they had to wage war to the death on the bear. In principle this was justified but it was an exaggeration.

Once on a fishing expedition I had the opportunity of a rare sight. I was asleep on a bed of straw in a small logging camp when the guide, who had risen at dawn and gone out to get some sun and fresh air, came in without making a sound and woke me up. 'What's going on?' I asked in a voice heavy with sleep. 'Quick, come and see. Quick!' he replied. With almost no clothes on I followed him, and there, thirty feet away, a black bear, enormous, sitting up on his haunches, took a look at us for a few seconds, then, no doubt more frightened than we

were ourselves, bounded to his feet and went off like lightning, back by the path he had come from. At the same moment a female moose from nobody knows where went off in pursuit and thumped his behind with kicks that made him groan like a child. Soon afterwards we came on the explanation of this unusual fracas. The mama moose was defending her baby. On the fresh earth of the undergrowth there was the tiny hoof-mark of a newborn moose. The guide, turning to me, said: 'I've been travelling through the woods for forty years now and I've never seen anything like it.'

THE BEAVER AND OTHER ANIMALS

I am proud of the fact that I was the first Canadian journalist to make known to Quebec the existence of Grey Owl and his self-appointed mission of protecting our fauna from the excesses of the hunt. Thanks to a young Rivière-du-Loup notary, I had discovered him in a Témiscouata forest. He had settled down with his charming and very beautiful wife Anahareo, a native American Indian, in a deserted cabin that had belonged to a lumberjack.

There he played the sympathetic host several times a day to a pair of beavers that he had

179

completely tamed and that he let go free in the lake opposite. There I witnessed charming scenes between man and beast.

Grey Owl passed for an authentic American Indian. He had the features and wore the dress. In fact he was a highly cultivated Englishman, a poet and thinker. The world long ago forgave him for the hoax he perpetrated because of the work of conservation he tried to accomplish. What he wanted to do – this man who loved nature to the point of sacrificing everything for it, even his name – was to spare wild animals from useless slaughter, to awaken in men pity for and interest in them, to teach men how to know and love them better.

At that time and from the first days of colonial rule life had been hard for the beavers. For a long time their thick, warm fur had been very important in the economic life of this country. Grey Owl felt that it was too heavy a tribute to pay to feminine and even masculine vanity (do you remember the beaver hats?). He considered beaver on a level with our pedigreed dogs and cats except that he found the beaver more intelligent.

The lot of the beaver has improved since then, but it is not certain that this is due to Grey

Owl's campaign. The animal's fur has greatly depreciated in value on the world market in the last quarter century. Skins sell much cheaper and the trapper has lost interest, perhaps because hunting beaver in the depths of winter is rugged work.

The result then is that the animal has been entirely free to reproduce and some are found everywhere. He makes his presence known by the ingenious dams that he builds across our rivers or at the outlets of lakes – often annoying when the rising water floods main paths or even highways. Sometimes the dams become a serious nuisance and must be demolished.

Even so, we have to admire the beavers for the way they fell great trees and cut them up with their sharp teeth, for their incredible skill in blocking the rushing course of a stream with small logs, and for the way they store a supply of poplar branches underneath the water as food for the winter.

In the warm months one enormous beaver makes several trips to explore the shore under the windows of our summer home in the Laurentians. I wish that I had the talent and patience of a Grey Owl to tame him and make a friend of him.

How many other Quebec animals there are worthy of notice! In certain parts of the country deer are plentiful, especially along the Canadian-American border throughout the Eastern Townships to the edges of Témiscouata County; but as they are to be found in all of North America we give them only brief attention. All summer they live contentedly in the vicinity of farm-houses and farms because they have doubtless learned that hunting is prohibited at that time of year. But when autumn comes and they hear the first shots, they avoid man, who has suddenly become the enemy, and usually escape the pursuing hunter. With the first snows, however, a number of deer fall under the murderous shooting because they can no longer hide their tracks. But enough of them survive in spite of everything to give us in spring the joy of watching elegant does with their spotted fawns.

Winter hunting is more a commercial enterprise than a sport. Courageous trappers set their traps in regions where game is most plentiful and come back with the fur of mink, silver fox, otter, raccoon, muskrat, ermine, lynx, marten, and so on. Sealskins from the far north are also much in demand. All of those animals – we have

given only a very incomplete list – make a living for some and contribute to the elegant attire of women. Hunting them is legitimate on condition that there is no revolting slaughter and that laws are observed.

BIRDS

Who has not heard of the Canada goose? These great birds, of the same family as the domestic goose that they resemble, invade our territories as soon as our lakes are open and make the journey in stages to the Arctic where they lay their eggs and raise their young.

CANADA GEESE IN FULL FLIGHT

Canada geese, heavier and fuller-bodied than the largest duck, fly in groups of around a hundred at an altitude of two miles. It is a flight in Vee formation that seems to have set the pattern for Air Force squadrons. First there is the leader, cleaving the air, with the whole troop trailing after, every flap of a wing seeming to be stressed with a hoarse cry; there also seems to be a captain who leaves the group at times as if to issue landing orders when the flock is ready to settle for the night. At the first signs of ice in autumn the same groups, with the year's young

added, will repeat the journey, this time from north to south.

A great number of these *outardes*, whose flesh is so tasty, are shot down as they pass through our Laurentian regions just before winter comes.

SNOW GEESE

Somewhat more rare, and more unusual, are the snow geese. These great white birds migrate in the same fashion as the *outardes*, except that all of them follow the same route from south to north and north to south. The spectacle that they offer is unique and exists, I believe, nowhere else on the planet.

After laying their eggs, hatching them, and then raising their young in Greenland, the snow geese migrate toward the United States, all stopping at the foot of Cape Tourmente a few miles from Quebec City. They number from twenty to twenty-five thousand. They will start south again only some weeks later. And in the interval they will gorge on a plant that apparently is essential to them.

For those Quebec people who have a permit, hunting these magnificent birds, which are very flavourful, is a royal sport. Surrounded by decoys and hidden in ditches about six feet deep, where they sit on wooden benches with something to keep them warm as well as good guns, the hunters await their prey. The snow geese fly over them in flocks of ten, twelve, or twenty. Then there will be a blast and several of the great birds fall to the ground like so many snowballs.

Every species of duck lives and multiplies on the many lakes of Quebec. At the time of migration in late autumn the ducks come in millions down to the waters of the St. Lawrence in the first stage of their long journey south. All along the great river hunters kill them in enormous numbers. People shoot them on the wing, taking aim at the flight. Trained dogs swim out to find the victims and bring them back to the feet of the master, who is huddled in a *cache*. This hunt takes endurance and sometimes a bottle of good gin. In cold October weather one has to crouch in a *cache* and wait there without moving for interminable quarter-hour periods for a flight willing to settle beside the decoys.

A PRETTY COUSIN OF THE ROOSTER

With minor exceptions there are no pheasants

in Quebec. On the other hand, grouse, which I shall call partridge because all Canadians call them that, abound in all our forests and on the wooded edges of cultivated fields. This is perhaps the prettiest of the gallinacious birds, with its aigrette on top of its head, its eye-marked plumage and fan-shaped tail. And nothing can compare with the taste of its flesh, which makes a main dish for a most sumptuous meal.

Do you want to have a fine, healthy, pleasant time? Around the end of September or the beginning of October on a sunny morning, put on some bright-coloured clothes so that a careless hunter will not mistake you for a deer and, carrying your gun, make your way along a winding path between two long rows of trees decked in autumn colours. Walk slowly and quietly. The bird that hears you coming will be impossible to catch if it has already been shot at. Look and listen; do not neglect any unusual sound, any movement in the bushes or high grass. A perfect mimic, the partridge is easily mistaken for a piece of log or a stump. Very often before you even see one you will be two feet away and it will be too late: your bird will fly off with a great fluttering of its wings and nine times out of ten it will be useless for you to follow. This is why, at the end of the day, if you have succeeded in bagging four or five partridges you may consider yourself a good hunter. Later on when the January cold keeps you at home, you will remember the fine birds you outwitted and even those you missed.

A word must be said about the small birds that exist, one might say, only to delight the eye and ear of man. The list of them is so long it would fill a book. There is no land richer in winged creatures of all kinds. Around every house in the country and even in city gardens you will see almost every sort of plumage and hear almost every song. According to the region and the time of year and with a little watching one can quickly identify finches, warblers, swallows, blackbirds, robins, orioles, bluejays, waxwings, goldfinches, mockingbirds, meadowlarks, magpies, snipes, woodpeckers, and a hundred other interesting species.

To these charming guests one should without doubt add the various kinds of falcons (some of which can be trained for the hunt), owls, and eagles. But for a complete picture of the birds of Quebec, even an immense fresco would not be big enough.

A People on the March

Nature in Quebec is appealing: the people who live in it and love it are even more appealing. One does not have to travel far in this vast territory to recognize how friendly they are, how hospitable, always ready to give information or to be of service. Most of the people you will meet here will be French-speaking, since these make up more than eighty per cent of the population. You will admire not only their fidelity to a language and to a culture but everywhere an awakening to contemporary realities.

Canadians of French origin intend to use, in the service of this land that was discovered, developed, and peopled by their forefathers, everything that modern science has to offer for its enrichment so that it may be the equal of any part of North America. They also intend to co-operate actively in promoting the growth and progress of the Canadian nation and are going about it in a way to compel recognition through the fruitfulness of their efforts and the excellence of a culture adapted to their times.

191

192

194

195

197

*Photographs of special interest
or unique scenes
are described below*